LETTERS TO MOTHER

LETTERS TO MOTHER

NARENDRA MODI

Translated from the Gujarati
Saakshi Bhaav by
BHAWANA SOMAAYA

HarperCollins *Publishers* India

First published in Gujarati as *Saakshi Bhaav* by
Image Publications 2014
First published in hardback in English in India by
HarperCollins *Publishers* 2020
4th Floor, Tower A, Building No. 10, DLF Cyber City,
DLF Phase II, Gurugram, Haryana – 122002
www.harpercollins.co.in

This edition published by HarperCollins *Publishers* 2024

2 4 6 8 10 9 7 5 3 1

P-ISBN: 978-93-6213-651-0
E-ISBN: 978-93-5357-633-2

Typeset in 12/17 Adobe Jenson Pro at
HarperCollins *Publishers* India

Printed and bound at
Replika Press Pvt. Ltd.

MIX
Paper | Supporting responsible forestry
FSC™ C016779
FSC www.fsc.org

CONTENTS

PUBLISHER'S NOTE

The pieces that make up this book go back thirty-four years: they were written in 1986. A party worker at the time, Narendra Modi had got into the habit of writing a letter to the Mother Goddess, whom he addressed as *Jagat janani*, every night before going to bed. In his jottings he revealed his innermost feelings, thoughts and doubts.

But every few months, he would tear up the pages of his journal and consign them to a bonfire. The pages of one diary, however, survived. These are now available in English for the very first time as *Letters to Mother*, in a powerful translation by Bhawana Somaaya.

Acknowledgements

Our gratitude to Image Publishers for sharing *Saakshi Bhaav* with us, and to Bhakti Desai Shetty.

FOREWORD

This is not an attempt at literary writing; the passages featured in this book are reflections of my observations and sometimes unprocessed thoughts, expressed without filters.

A public figure is always judged by his position; irrespective of what he says or does, his persona becomes so exaggerated that it is difficult to trace the man behind the image or, let me put it this way, there comes a time when there is no desire in us to search for the individual behind the mask.

To live an ordinary life is a privilege and deep within, all of us are but ordinary mortals affected by the positive and the negative showering bestowed upon us by the universe. None of us are above vices, virtues, hope, disappointment, love, yearning, expectations or ambitions.

Like you, I am an ordinary mortal with some strengths and some weaknesses, and like everyone, I am constantly struggling to become more aware and evolved.

Sometime in the past when the pressures became insurmountable, I got into the habit of writing letters to the Mother Goddess, whom I address as *Jagat janani*. I shared my innermost thoughts with her every night before going to bed, and this exercise had a strangely calming effect on me. I looked forward to everyone falling asleep, so that I could retire to a quiet corner with my notebook.

The intention was never to get published, the jottings were for myself. I am not a writer, most of us are not; but everybody seeks expression, and when the urge to unload becomes overpowering there is no option but to take pen to paper, not necessarily to write but to introspect and unravel what is happening within the heart and the head, and why. The exercise proved cathartic, and even though it was a one-way communication with the Mother Goddess, the discipline of rewinding my daily thoughts healed me in a strange, unique way, like I was being shielded by a bigger force.

I wrote every single night, for years; and every few months, I systematically tore up all the pages and threw them into a bonfire. I have lost count of the number of pages I have consigned to the flames. Then one day, while I was in the process of igniting the flames, my dear friend and respected colleague from the RSS, Narendra *bhai* Panchsara visited my home unannounced. He was led to the garden where I was busy tearing up sheets of paper. Panchsara *bhai* snatched the remaining pages from my hand. He was angry and admonished me for destroying my valuable jottings, emphasizing the importance of documentation. 'That you wrote them and preserved them all this while is proof that these are precious to you; to destroy them is to disrespect your instinct,' he said.

His words impacted me and I promised him that I would revere my instinct and stop lighting my quarterly bonfire. Years went by and one day, I still don't know how, Image Publishers got wind of my journal and wrote to me seeking my permission to publish these writings as a book. I declined, but once again it was Panchsara *bhai* who insisted I agree to the offer – probably because he feared that if they weren't published, I might try to destroy the pages again! The remains of those diary pages comprise *Saakshi Bhaav*, which was published in the year 2014.

I owe these letters and the book to my respected friend Panchsara *bhai*: had he not visited me that day, had he not intervened, had he not admonished and awakened me, I would have lost the opportunity of sharing my intimate conversations with the *Jagat janani*, wherein I present her my innermost feelings of fear, sorrow and conflict, the ordinary feelings of an ordinary man. I'm aware that my expressions are often abstract; perhaps when the heart is overwhelmed the mind races faster than the hand on paper, and so, yes, my expressions are sporadic and at the same time overflowing. I am not a professional writer, I don't understand structures and formats, but I do understand emotions – and I write because I feel strongly and cannot contain myself at that moment.

The Mother Goddess understands this, I am sure; she does not judge me, does not grade me by my choice of words or phrases – it does not matter to her whether I write prose, poetry, essays or random thoughts. She understands my intent, understands what is expressed and also what is left unsaid. And if I understand all this, why did I destroy all that I created? The only logical explanation I can offer is that probably because it is painful to revisit suffering.

Today, however, I seek strength from memories, have faith that all the joyous moments will linger and that sorrows will wither away. If the mind is positive there's always hope. I love books and read a lot, I am attracted to art and culture, but I don't fancy myself as a litterateur. I was reluctant to get the Gujarati version of *Saakshi Bhaav* published but was coerced into it by close friends, and the English translation after six years is a pleasant surprise.

It feels strange to read what you wrote many years ago, because you are not the same person anymore and your circumstances are different too; and yet, it is all a part of you, your journey, and I will not shy away from my outpourings. I wrote then what I felt at the time and I write now what I feel today. People judged me then; people continue to judge me today. I wasn't seeking endorsement many years ago and I am not seeking validation today.

All of us are entitled to self-expression and that's exactly what I have done.

Narendra Modi

TRANSLATOR'S NOTE

Every book has a story and this one is no exception.

In the year 2014, *Saakshi Bhaav*, the Gujarati original of *Letters to Mother*, was released at a glittering function in Mumbai.

At that time, sitting in the auditorium and listening to the passionate speech by Prime Minister Narendra Modi, then the chief minister of Gujarat, I could never have imagined that I would one day translate his Gujarati book into English.

Six years passed by and *Saakshi Bhaav* got lost in my overcrowded bookshelf at home.

Then one day, a writer friend asked me why I was not metaphrasing any more language books and suggested that I translate our prime minister's poetry into English. It seemed like a far-fetched idea, but I searched for *Saakshi Bhaav* in my bookshelf and began reading.

It was a slow but worthwhile read and by the time I finished, I was stirred by the urgency of the writing. In the Foreword of the book the author shares what compelled him to write these pages in his diary; he says he wrote because he could not contain his anxiety.

I pondered for a few days if I wanted to go through the daunting task of transcreating his work; finally, what attracted me to the book was Narendra Modi's undisguised display of emotions: his courage to lay himself bare and share his innermost thoughts was moving.

The passages are raw and hurting, often uneven and unchiselled – but he is at ease with his imperfections because feelings have no formalities. With his defences completely down, he reflects on the purpose of life, ponders over the passage of time, deliberates on the merits of technology in our lives and wonders if gadgets can ever replace human contact. There is remorse over the death of a dream, regrets for our inability to preserve heritage and the excitement of making preparations for a large-scale *Shibir* in a cold desert. We are privy to his struggles, his celebrations, his inner turbulence and his heartaches.

He sits by the ocean, gazes at the skyline, flies with the birds, trails the sun and the moon and gauges their moods. In his writing there is pathos, wonderment, agony, attachment and meditation too. His outpourings reflect his innumerable challenges and a brimming optimism to overcome all obstacles.

Sometimes you feel weighed down by his intense churnings and you wonder if he overthinks, feels a bit too strongly, and why. Is it possible for someone as preoccupied as him to contemplate on what appears apparently trivial? Doesn't the exercise drain him? Also, where does he find the inspiration to bounce back every time? Does this have to do with his roots, his adolescent years spent in the mountains? His mind is ticking all the time and he conjures images with his words, at times bold and breathtaking, and sometimes hauntingly morbid.

There is a simmering sorrow, an overwhelming gratitude towards the universe; he bequeaths disappointments, beckons aspirations; there is acute restlessness and euphoria as well, and there is a burning passion to usher in change, to create a utopian world. And that is the best part of the book: it is not written by the public figure he is today but an ordinary party worker during the 1980s, precisely the reason why the Foreword has been updated as well.

Letters to Mother is a transcreation of *Saakshi Bhaav*, rather it is an effort to capture the essence of the celebrity author. In the last six years, a lot has changed in the life of Narendra Modi, the prime minister of our country. It is natural for readers to search for the leader in his vintage writings. I did too; sometimes I located him, and sometimes, when images of daily news blurred with sepia footage, I lost him... And the intrigue continues.

The most appealing thing about the book is the author's connect with the universe, with the Mother Goddess; he has unflinching faith that she will hold his hand and walk him through the roughest terrain, and probably she does. *Letters to Mother* is his intimate and unfiltered conversations with the deity and reveals that the most powerful people are human too.

Bhawana Somaaya

At times,
Life appears a tomb of dreams
Ushering speed and thought
And at times,
A ruin of dreams
Soaked in tears

PURPOSE OF LIFE

1ST DECEMBER 1986

The first day of the last month
Of the year 1986
The still calendar on the wall
An indicator of time
Ironical, isn't it?

Human life is a constant
While the universe is about speed
So, where do I fit into all this?
Do I move with pace?
Do I challenge it?

Is progress free movement
Or a mere illusion of movement
Am I also like the calendar on the wall?
Motionless,
Yet creating an illusion of movement?

Or is it that because there is life,
There is movement...
And how can one be certain
That this movement is positive?

And who determines the guidelines?
Of pace, of progress, of deterioration
Isn't it all subjective?
For what is progress for one
Often proves unfavourable to another

Then is life to be experienced
Only by what is apparent?
Can time ever be objective?
And if life is to be restricted
By the visible boundaries
Who is going to douse
These flames of discontentment?

Discontentment...
Triggered by deep reflection
And if one understands this
Shouldn't objectivity
Become the motto of our life?
Then why is it so difficult
To overcome attachment?

At times,
Life appears a tomb of dreams
Ushering speed and thought
And at times,
A ruin of dreams
Soaked in tears

And therefore
I wish for a life
Filled with compassion
Devoid of expectations
I yearn for it,
Rather implore for it

Punish this body if you have to
Break it into pieces
I will not cringe
But tell me, mother
Is it fair to bruise me thus?

DEBRIS OF DREAMS

2ND DECEMBER 1986

The sun rises every morning
With a purpose
But this morning
The sun appears hazy
Somewhat restless
As if something unbecoming
Is going to occur
Something macabre

It feels as if something precious
Is going to be stolen away from me
Strange, fearful thoughts hound me
As the sun hovers ominously

The body is here, the mind elsewhere
Why cannot the sun bridge
This body with my mind?
When I am here, the mind wanders
When the mind is here, I depart

Within moments, this mind flees
Long distances

Gallops without maps
Without lanterns
Fearless, without apprehensions
The mind sways, swaggers

Uncaring of this body
What it endures
Or how it blisters
In this churning of dreams

Then transforming into the moon
The mind gently embraces the body
In quietude
At times burns it too
Then the flames engulf
The entire universe in its folds

Dreams crumble into ruins
And everything turns futile...
Foggy, uneasy
You've sensed that, mother, haven't you?

Why is today so forbidding?
Why does the rising sun
Burn me with unbearable pain?
I can sense it, feel it, mother
With your blessings

The mind is numb today
A discomforting feeling
Of something ravaged
Something destroyed
Something wrecked
Of too much happening around me

Am I overreacting, hallucinating?
I don't think so, mother

Quietly, dreams return to roots
Quietly, expectations accept defeat
Quietly, the heart axes desires

The helplessness persists
As if every moment

Is dragging me to the end
I am absolutely certain
That it is the morning sun
That burns me!
Or doesn't it?

The moon visits later than usual
And without her mellow mood
Also, why does it keep me awake?
Must I endure so much suffering?

Punish this body if you have to
Break it into pieces
I will not cringe
But tell me, mother
Is it fair to bruise me thus?
When I've submitted to life, to you?

Or is it because
Just as every moment
Of my life is precious
Every moment is precious as well
And this moment has extinguished!

Pain of the past pierces my heart
Recreates images of torment
I grapple to overcome self-doubt
Why am I so faltering today?
Why is this heart so full of chaos?

Mother, do you refrain to warn me
Because you want to protect me
Because you don't want to make
This precious life unendurable

I want you to know
That I am prepared every moment
So why have you lost trust in me?
Lost faith in my ability to accept
Embrace and adapt to every situation?

Mother, please clarify
What arouses the dark clouds today?
I can sense the unforeseen
Because you reside within me
And if you know that as well
Why this uncertainty about my strength?

Or is it that you want me to be in this state?
Probably that is what you indicate
Or that is what I comprehend as of now

I lack courage to go against you
But I can plead, mother
That let whatever has to occur, unfold
And in the interim
You will experience
My sacrifice, my submission
Here, there, everywhere

As of now all situations
Rests in the embryo of the future
I want to submit all to you
And become carefree!

For the first time,
I sense thoughts
That words fear to express

And amidst all this the moon
Breezes past leaving a trail of fire

Mother, will tomorrow's sunrise
Prove as inauspicious?
It feels so now
There's hardly any time for dawn

A few moments perhaps...
And the sun knows this
Everything is numb...
Words, feelings, everything

It is your mercy, mother
That I'm able to connect
With the Oneness
And the reason,
I yearn to preserve your integrity

YOUR CREATION

3RD DECEMBER 1986

It feels as if I am hit by a cyclone
The morning sun, like yesterday
Circulates the universe and misleads
This quest for well-being remains a
dream
As they say:
Time heals all sorrows
And the rush of life ushers change
In surroundings
Perhaps
But will the chaos within me ever
subside?
I am not certain
Mother, the mere thought of making an
effort
Is daunting

A wave of thoughts raises questions
about life
Isn't life a poem created by you?
The lows and the highs are your mercy,
mother

Or are these apparent dormant disbeliefs
A ploy to validate your supremacy?

If I have unflinching faith in life
Then why am I unable to submit
To changing circumstances
Why do I resist the surprises at different curves?
Why do all of us desire a life only of our imagination?

Is it because life offers choices?
Because we submit to what prevails
As the will of the Almighty
Can our generosity be a façade for cowardice?
A defence mechanism to safeguard oneself
To glorify such mindset as buoyancy
Is to delude oneself and our loved ones

Then is life only about exploitation?
If so, how do we preserve our virtues?
How do we conquer our misgivings?
Is this the reason we are doomed to
darkness?

Can such hypocrisy ever
Lead to eternal happiness?
An evolvement that is distorted...
Can neither bring prestige nor retain
identity

In any case in this large universe
How many can man fool and for how
long?
How many costumes can he change?
On the stage of life
Is this then his final exit, definitely not!

Trusting your prowess, I state:
The veils will drop,

The masks will fall
Perhaps the universe will endure
But will certainly not accept

It is your mercy, mother
That I'm able to connect
With the Oneness
And the reason,
I yearn to preserve your integrity

The heart cries:
Why make life into a compromise
When it can be determination!
Only the supreme must have our
submission
Only then can we experience bliss
At least that's what I aspire for

Oh mother, free me from this bondage
Liberate me, empower me to assess people

Beyond masks, beyond words
I don't want to judge
Don't want to exert my superiority

I want to decipher the right from the
wrong
This is imperative for my growth
I want to extend my strength beyond self
Bless me, mother
That I am never unjust to others
And if injustice crosses my path
I have the strength to confront

Look at me, mother
I am like the ever-bankrupt trader
Seeking new loans, your blessings
All the time
You are the provider, the protector
About that I am certain

I want to light lamps
In every feeble, dreamless eye
I want to ignite speed
Into all drained, standstill feet
I want to shake up the silent ocean
Row oars of passion
Into the quietly flowing waves

MOTHER GODDESS

5TH DECEMBER 1986

Parched fields
Blistered earth
Clouds gather
Raising hopes
When suddenly
A storm intervenes
Clouds disperse
Without a drizzle
Torturous moment

Time for kids to return from school
Mother waits by the window
Her eyes anxious
Feet rush inside-outside doors
But the gaze is fixed at the gate
Ears perked up to hear 'mother'
The slightest delay in their arrival
Adds anxiety, makes her restless

The pounding heart can shatter walls
As feet stagger helter-skelter
And eyes brim with apprehension
Separation turns to agony

Yes, that's the effect of waiting
Somewhat like life

Perhaps there's a difference in passion
Perhaps in expression
Perhaps like a new bride
Their pain of waiting is constrained
Perhaps...

Moments of anticipation are beacons
Of our attachments
The ups and the downs we encounter
Our barometers of intensity
Like the streams gushing into the ocean
We sway and rock in the rhythm
Overflowing, extending boundaries
At times scathing, often uneasy

Have you ever sat beneath
A blossoming tree
And experienced longing?
Every bark, every branch

Becomes a participant in your woe
Bending, curling, swathing you
In its compassion
Sensing your anxiety while waiting
They become anxious too!

And
When the waiting concludes
When you meet the person, you desire
Then –

If you can, do rise above self
And gaze at those dancing flowers
The singing leaves
The swaying branches
All firmly held together
By the robust trunk

To experience this
You have to covet
Intense longing
Initiate tireless efforts

Towards an enriching journey
And the reason why waiting
Is more agonizing than parting

Mother, I relish residing
In this passion-driven universe
But fear at times if my yearnings
Will obstruct my growth
Or maybe passion finds its path
Because God-gifted love
Cannot be so restricted
That I cannot share with others
Cannot drench my loved ones
In its fragrance

I want to connect
With the feelings of all
I want to absolve
The sufferings of all
I want to surrender
Submit to all
Therefore, I wonder

Why am I not consumed
By this eternally burning passion?

Can you see, mother
How the moment of waiting
Torments me?
Is it necessary that every churning
Yield positive results?
If that is so, how is it selfless?

I want to be empowered
To be able to touch every soul
Sow seeds of love,
Sprout happiness
Inside every parched heart

I want to light lamps
In every feeble, dreamless eye
I want to ignite speed
Into all drained, standstill feet
I want to shake up the silent ocean
Row oars of passion
Into the quietly flowing waves

Mother...
I wait for total submission
I wait for infinite growth
I wait to be self-contained
To be drenched in emotions
To splash in the rain like a child
And live for the moment

Mother...
I have no requests
No favours to seek
I just desire to embrace
This universe full of love
I envision this wondrous existence
Not for self
But in association with you
And therefore yearn
For the ardent belongings

I accept the pain of waiting
The agony makes me stronger
The silence accompanying grief

Is meditative
The surrounding darkness
Is self-created
The associated discomfort
My fatal attraction

This waiting is out of my desire
And therefore, I have no complaints
Towards any moment bestowed by you
But yes, one thing stays unexpressed
Why do you not silence
The ongoing chaos within me

Do you avoid clarification, mother
For you fear truth will drown me?
Or is the hesitation out of concern
To protect another
If that is so
Don't you know your own better?
That you are the root of my being...
So why propel me
With compelling circumstances today?

Mother, liberate me
From doubts, disappointments
From fears and anxieties
From triumphs and defeats
From possession, from loss
Free me from all forever

When I am clairvoyant
Why this uncertainty?
Why has our conscience
Become slave to a fractured society?
Or is this how life is meant to be lived?

The heart weeps
And there's no one to adhere to
Why do you abandon me?
What have I done, mother,
That you penalize me thus?
Why do you make me so powerless?
Or is this your way of testing me?

It is all your doing
Without you guarding me
Would I have survived this
biting cold?
Or write these words
Seated under this forest tent?
No specific subject, random
thoughts
Just a few worries, I guess

TENDER GAZE

6TH DECEMBER 1986

The world is becoming a small place
Man-created technology has reduced distances
We watch events across the universe
Sitting in our homes
And we love it

The small gadget ushers intimacy
But does it exercise discretion?
Can gadget-created intimacy become reality?
Or is it an illusion?
The thought suggests togetherness
Or is the thought a mere ploy?

Today, letter-writing is on a decline
Words no longer have a chance
To paint feelings on paper
And most essential,
History will hold no record of time gone by

At the same time, it is prudent
To undermine the importance of
technology
In present times
In a crowd when someone shouts 'hey
you'
It is natural to turn around
Because the 'I' within all of us is forever eager
That someone familiar seeks us amidst
strangers
Generates a feeling of elation—
And what if the call is not for you?
There is a change in expression
Can the telephone ever have the same
impact?

Sheer courtesy, at times
Transforms into a mode of
communication
Often words, voice, change of tone,
thoughts
Are inadequate to express sentiments

Don't animals have feelings?
Don't they express themselves?
Probably better than us humans
Through eyes, through touch
They connect with ease in silence

Their responses are spontaneous
Unlike us surviving in a hypocritical world
Our feelings have fractured to an extent
That we need support for expression
Why are we so forlorn, so defenceless?

Even a mother needs to rely
On exterior distractions like toys
To cheer and engage her child
Isn't she powerless as well?

The child comprehends no language
But responds to tender gaze, touch
Eyes are a powerful medium of connection

They reveal what's going on inside the heart
Without words, just a glance is sufficient
To penetrate deep within the soul

Will this universe in pursuit of technology
Lose the treasures gifted by nature?
Can anything be more precious
Than the expression in the eyes?

Eyes restrain, control tears
When the heart overflows
And yet
Even strangers gauge something is amiss
What is this connection?

Does waiting follow a vocabulary?
They reflect every passing moment
Also, moments to come...
They express physical agony better

Than powerful, piercing words
They complain in silence

Did we follow, study any books
To grasp these expressions
And yet, everybody all over the universe
Across language, across cultures,
comprehends it
A mystery isn't it?

When we are blessed with such strong
Natural means of communication
It's unfortunate that we depend
On outer sources for expression
Particularly since this outer source
Is inadequate to absorb the complexity
Of myriad, mixed emotions

Here I am harping on my feelings
And ways of expressing them
While echoes of celebrations

Around me are in full swing
Supporters from all over the country
Are filtering in at the *Shibir*

Mother, we have put our best efforts
In our arrangements to host them
So many volunteers, young and old
Have worked day and night
Tirelessly
Cheerfully
Enthusiastically
To facilitate the guests

In their service to the nation
There is an endeavour to boost
confidence
To be inspired
Their eyes brim over with devotion
For society, for *Sangh* and for nation
Their sincerity is overwhelming

I need to acknowledge your contribution
My dear mother
If you had not blessed me with
benevolence
Would I have embraced life
wholeheartedly?

It is all your doing
Without you guarding me
Would I have survived this biting cold?
Or write these words
Seated under this forest tent?
No specific subject, random thoughts
Just a few worries, I guess

The restlessness to dream
For a prosperous nation
The ambition to expand
From the minuscule
To the magnitude
Of combining
Discipline with institution

SUPREME CONFIDENCE

7TH DECEMBER 1986

Mother, I am truly blessed
It has been four days since
I have eaten or slept
In part due to circumstances
In part out of my own resolution
But I don't sense exhaustion

Last night passed without a blink
Still the heart is filled with joy
Is this possible
Without your blessings?

All night,
Volunteers drove in large numbers
And at the crack of dawn
We inaugurated the *Shibir*
What an unusual ambience
The tent was a novel experience for many
And appreciated

Sometimes, mother, I feel
That it's better if words don't come true

You will take care of that, won't you?
This time again, it was the same story
My estimate of expected volunteers
Was different from the rest

Yes, the arrangements were in order
But the total number I predicted came
true
The aggregate of *Swayam Sevaks*
With difficulty added up to nine hundred

With your blessings
There is no dearth of enthusiasts
It is another matter that their excitement
Doesn't always yield the promised results

Youth is in celebration here
Assembled in the bristling cold
To joyously work together
They are aware of the lack of facilities
Yet are full of cheer

There is faith and therefore a possibility
There is commitment to motherland
And their determination remains
unbroken

When disappointment engulfs from all
sides
The young, the old and the children
Instill faith in victory
In their chosen path, chosen thought
In their acquired governance
They exhibit unflinching affection
Isn't that amazing?

Does anyone tutor them these lessons of
love?
Can the intimacy experienced
Be a means to an end of personal
anguish?
Is there a language for this barter?
No, because love is the essence of life

Encompassing and touching us every moment

Then, is this a process of evolution
From self to all
An ongoing, continuous exercise
Where self is a mere instrument
To empower the mind
A process of collective acceptance?

For it is only when you rise above self
Mobilizing everyone around you
That your journey becomes
Fruitful, fragrant

It is only when you submit
Without reservations
That you experience eternal bliss!
And this deposit of undiluted joy
In my opinion, is the result of
Complete union
When you encounter
Supreme confidence

The restlessness to dream
For a prosperous nation
The ambition to expand
From the minuscule
To the magnitude
Of combining
Discipline with institution

It is the beginning of a new journey
Without bondage of penance
Without shrine of worship
As Vivekananda said:
The fulfilment of desire
Of the downtrodden
Is the only truth and real power

Yes, from here will sprout
A blossoming life
From here will shine
A radiant light
From here will bloom
A quest for divinity
The new union

Will sow new seeds of hope
Weave new dreams
For the naked eye

This is life and therefore
Every eye holds a dream
Every heart burns a flame
Let's see, how many hearts
Can this flame ignite?

So many queries...
Or should I say so many
expectations of me!
Mother, will I be able to fulfil
them all?
Will I hold true of their faith
in me?
With dedicated hard work
Will I accomplish the promise?
I sense immense trust
But also, high expectations

THE HEART IS A TEMPLE

8TH DECEMBER 1986

Today is the second day of *Shibir*
Of a breathless schedule of organizing
There is excitement all around
Eyes filled with anticipation
At the sheer thought of
Spending two purpose-filled days

Today, the chief guest is expected
No special welcome is planned in his honour
He arrives just like the rest
Yet his sheer presence spreads an aura
Fills the volunteers with excitement

They watch his every move
Hang on to his every word
There is an eagerness to connect
And every one present here
Feels the same way

For me this is a unique experience
After assuming new responsibility

I'm meeting respected Bala Saheb
For the first time
On arrival at the *Shibir*
His first question to me:
So, how's your new domesticity shaping up?

I am surprised
For a man as busy as him to remember
What does it reflect?
Once we begin chatting of course
There is an avalanche of questions:

What is the police report?
What do the media say?
Did you make a public address?
If not, why so?
So many queries...
Or should I say so many expectations of me!

Mother, will I be able to fulfil them all?
Will I hold true of their faith in me?

With dedicated hard work
Will I accomplish the promise?
I sense immense trust
But also, high expectations

Today, Gujarat is the cynosure of all eyes
The entire nation is focused
On our novel experiment
I wonder if I will be able to rise
To meet their perception of me

Not a step is possible
Without your intervention, mother
Sometimes I too reflect
On the immediate gains and losses
Sometimes I ponder over
The frequent lapses in conduct

Do I make an adequate effort?
To evolve myself
There is a constant endeavour
In that direction

But am I always able to
Gauge the larger perspective?

Do I comprehend the collective voice?
If not, will there not be repercussions?
Mother, I must sense a storm within me
But that storm hasn't unleashed as yet

All speculations regarding my new role
Have more or less settled down
The surprise, the distrust has quietened
Now begin the expectations
Myriad, manifold, intense assumptions
The beginning of a new role in life

I am ready for an endless struggle
Ready to bestow my journey of fifteen
years
This is a challenge to carry forward
A legacy of ideologies

With your blessings, mother
I know I will pass the test
Time has come to finally live the life
We have so far watched through
binoculars

It isn't easy coming close to your dream
I'm fearful of breaking illusions
Fearful of lifting the veil
Dusting off the long-accumulated rusted
Baggage of intense likes and dislikes

I accept the challenge
And I seek your blessings
Fill me with strength
Fill me with faith
That I don't crumble
In my commitment

Today was a gruelling day
But Bala Saheb was so inspiring

So many *Swayam Sevaks* meeting him
For the first time
And all of them were ecstatic

There was no time for any daily routine
Today
No correspondence
No responses to letters
So busy and preoccupied

How the world perceives me
Is of little significance to me
As long as this heart
Remains connected with you

INSPIRING NEW LIFE

9TH DECEMBER 1986

Today is the final day of the *Shibir*
Till yesterday we ran helter-skelter
Supervising the minutest detail
Today, we are in the process
Of deconstructing our efforts

Quite like life...
Transitory, meaningless
And yet we are unable to
Disconnect
With pain, with promise
Our quest, our perspective

Perhaps fulfilment ushers
Sporadic joys
Perhaps that is the conditioning
Perhaps it is the power of victory
But even power is transitory
And yet, mother
Everyone desires acquisition
I am no exception

This must not happen
If my foundation is adequate
If I am on the path of evolvement
Then I should be free
Of the narrow-minded mentality

Like the cyclone that uproots
And flings you to a faraway place
This vagabond heart is a victim
Of long-nursed ambitions
Long-lived dreams
Is there no way out of this?

Or is this the only way
Towards detachment
Perhaps seeking this path
Is our biggest turmoil

Today will prove a significant day
Today new roads
Will lead to new progress
New directions, new surroundings

Unfortunately, even this commences
With elections
Time for consciousness to sweep away
Life's dormant desires

The stream flows gently
Unlike the ocean
It lacks the capacity to absorb the planet
But is adequately equipped
To revive the barren earth
It has the capacity to spread cheer
To sing songs
To touch our hearts
To offer us solace

It is not as vast as the ocean
Has not endured storms like the sea
Nor battled floods like the river
Is soundless, unobtrusive
Devoid of force or speed
Yet is self-contained!

It carves an impression on us
Despite its fragile frame
Its fragrance is inspiring
It is beyond expectations
Content and consistent in flow

Mother, this is the absolute truth
Yet, I'm set to swim against the tide
I am drawn to the chaos
With a calm, meditative mind

Mother, I know this body
Is ready for another platform
For a new costume, a new role
The mind, body, heart and soul
Presented in adequate packaging

With your blessings, mother
This will happen too
And there again,
I will raise awareness
This body-heart-intellect

Are pledged to consciousness
And it is this mindfulness
That connects my soul to you

How the world perceives me
Is of little significance to me
As long as this heart
Remains connected with you
Consistently
Passionately
Perhaps it is my faith in you
That shields me from the worst crises

Mother, today was the meeting
I spoke little,
Felt alone amidst a crowd
The heart overflowed with
sorrow
Then why was I unable to
express it, mother?

Mercurial Time

10TH December 1986

Like a bird's nest broken
Everything has gone awry
Till yesterday,
This was a sacred place
Where several hearts united
To meditate
Today, it appears disarrayed
As if swept away by floods

If I had the provisions, mother
I would have preserved every joy
Measure by measure and treasured
The fun-filled times forever

Anyway, it is all part of life
Sometimes euphoria
Sometimes gloom
Time I get accustomed to all
A difficult phase indeed
So many different encounters

At times celebrations
At times desolation
At times waiting
At times farewell
Sometimes dialogues
Sometimes deliberations
So many mixed sentiments

As hope alternates with disappointments
I feel torn in two different directions

Is it possible that this scattered state
Is the beginning of a new creation?
Is it possible that this inner conflict
Will define a new direction of time?
Only time will lay the foundation
And determine the strength, stature
Of a new structure

Mother, today was the meeting
I spoke little,

Felt alone amidst a crowd
Voiced concern for the famine victims
But not sure if my argument made impact
My presentation was devoid of
Pain, pathos, anger or assertion
I wonder why
The heart overflowed with sorrow
Then why was I unable to express it,
mother?

Can it be true that when man
Becomes self-absorbed
Is the time when his outer life
Starts to wind up for him?
Mother, with your blessings
I aspire to retain all my attachments
I want to feel the same compassion
For everyone around me forever

Mother, I also desire
To conquer time
To seize moments of life
I want you to drop
The time-dew
That will pave my path
And till that happens
I will float through life
Waiting to find it
Sometime, somewhere

TIME TRAVELS

21ST DECEMBER 1986

Sometimes
Time tiptoes out of the room
Sometimes,
It spreads like a rock
On my chest
Weighs me down with its burden

I wasn't aware
That time has thorns
It pokes and pierces
Bruises and bleeds this heart

Sometimes
Time is fragrant too
And gently, smoothly passes by
Exits without remnants of aroma
Without touch, without signs!

Man has forever trapped time
Within the hands of the clock
Assembled it in small

Structures and machines
And yet sometimes, somewhere
Time must feel restricted
In its quietude
In its stillness
In its pace

Such moments stand still
Untouched and preserved
Like a statue
Sometimes visible
At times invisible

How many such moments
In our lives
In our society
In our nation
Can we describe as immortal?

Perhaps, such moments
In an individual's life
Remain unexpressed

The intensity however
Remains unmistakable

Something similar occurs
Within the human heart
When a solitary dew drop
Isolated from gushing rain
Seeks shelter deep inside us
As within an oyster
Transforms into a precious pearl
And becomes immortal

But for this to occur
The heart must overflow with love
The outcry laced with tremor
The quest so intense that it scathes
The flame so severe that it burns
The past, present and the future

Where everything is entwined
And entangled
Where eyes view from the soul

And ears echo their own drums
Where nerve-ends meet collectively
Such moments alone transform
Time into the immortal

Time needs to be paused
Time needs to take shape
At times it needs to
Endure suffering, euphoria
At times, time needs to
Get overwhelmed

Mother, I also desire
To conquer time
To seize moments of life
I want you to drop
The time-dew
That will pave my path

And till that happens
I will float through life
Waiting to find it
Sometime, somewhere

To create
You need deafening silence
You need to absorb the
magnitude
Of the horizon within you
You need to look within you
Your eyes wide open

CREATING OUT OF A VACUUM

22ND DECEMBER 1986

There appears to be a paucity
Of poetry
Like the famine in Gujarat
Sometimes there is production
But not creation for sure

The process of production is
To add raw material into the can
Fill it up to the brim
Then press the button

If the machine is pen or pencil
Drop blocks of alphabets in
Watch them take shape
Into collective words
Gradually
Depending on their potential
The words will extend into
Long sentences

When the raw material exhausts
So does the production!
Production is a continuous process
It is unfortunate that most of us
Mistake production for creation

Because
Those accustomed
To rearing children on powder milk
Will never understand creation

To create
You need deafening silence
You need to absorb the magnitude
Of the horizon within you
You need to look within you
Your eyes wide open

No search for words
No symphony of alphabets
Whether the heart is joyous
Or it is in mourning

The intensity rages
Hits you like the ocean
The salty waves hurt
Your eyes, your tongue
And you let out a scream

What if the same lashes
Your heart?
Then the ocean dives within you
And you rock the boat of words
Without oars

Such extreme moments
Sometimes
Become the cradle of creation

Earlier man exploited man
Now he exploits religion
Mother,
I want to embrace mankind
With all the failings
And without expectations
Give me the strength
That I'm able to accomplish it

THIS IS THE ONLY PATH

23RD DECEMBER 1986

Dawn to dusk
Is an opportunity
To meet and acquaint with
So many different people

But how many of us
Really connect with their hearts?
How many of us
Nurture an appetite for bonding?

It is confusing, can it be
That man has got lost
Hunting a reflection of self?
Or is it that
Just as he uses gadgets
For his convenience
He exploits people
To his advantage?

Everywhere you look
The anguished heart cries

Everywhere
Is an indication of gloom!

Man searches
For he senses a vacuum within
He aspires to acquire
But the more he acquires
The more he dreams
And the wheel continues

And for this ongoing exercise
We have invented a silken name
Relationships –
At times, intimate
At times, not so formal
Sometimes a friend
Sometimes a beloved

In a vortex of words
Man sponges off man
For vested interest

To fulfil a goal
That's it

In pursuit of power
He wears a cloak
In a facade of submission
He aspires to capture more

Mother, will the human heart
Continue to be so cruel?
Will man never lead a simple
Uncomplicated, unbiased
Tender, tranquil existence
Devoid of expectations?
Is it that difficult to resolve
The conflict?

Contentment is the essence of life
And if he cannot in this state
Embrace life in all forms and phases
Then where will all this end?

Today, he no more makes an effort
To rise above ego, to break free
From the self-created illusory world

Then is life only about self-serving?
Is that the reason why in his later years
He is drawn to religion?
Or is it that he weaves a web of deceit
To retain his mirage?

He makes every possible effort
To preserve his persona
He poses, pretends
In the guise of giving
He plots to acquire
And the reason
Why in his later years
He seeks religion
Is to shield himself

Earlier man exploited man
Now he exploits religion

Mother,
I want to embrace mankind
With all the failings
And without expectations
Give me the strength
That I'm able to accomplish it
Without any give and take
Without the trap of words

Mother, I have nothing to prove
Just wish to submit myself
Without barter, without fear
It is the only way towards
Higher attainment
Because for me,
Man can never be a commodity

You are determined to torment me
And I seem destined for
suffering
Still I have faith in my integrity
I know, I will someday
Court the circumstances I
deserve
Mother,
I have submitted to you
What more can I do?

ANGUISHED CRY

25TH DECEMBER 1986

Feeling upbeat since morning
The energy dusts away my physical
fatigue
Wish I could do the same with my mental
worries
But this is possible only if you will it,
mother

And yet
Deep within, I hear anguished cries
Why does the mind resemble
The ravages of 3rd and 4th December
The day passes in distractions
But the fear persists

Is something odd occurring around me?
I sense something ominous
Something robbed, something stolen

Mother, a series of questions
Sprout in the heart, create a web
These queries aren't without reason

This piercing agony in the heart
Is not without foundation

For sure, this is a sign from you
I know it
Yet I am but mortal
Getting weaker day by day
Not always adequate
To decode your signals, mother

So, must I suffer this churning?
I sense something forbidding
I anticipate what is to unfold
Will be undesirable
But must you create so much intrigue?

You are determined to torment me
And I seem destined for suffering
Still I have faith in my integrity
I know, I will someday
Court the circumstances I deserve
Mother,
I have submitted to you
What more can I do?

Why is it that
Despite my immense suffering
There is no trace of creation?
Then is it compassion not
anguish
That compels creation?

PAIN IS NOT AN ORPHAN

28TH DECEMBER 1986

Unbearable anguish
Insurmountable surroundings
It is said that in every creation
You sense the suffering of the creator

Then why is it that
Despite my immense suffering
There is no trace of creation?
Then is it compassion not anguish
That compels creation?
For pain is the after-effect of sorrow

Usually it is negativity
That ushers pain
Erodes your senses
And paralyzes you

Pain has no lineage
Its presence, growth, intensity
Is dependent on emotions
Therefore, pain isn't an orphan

Nor is pain always barren
There's no guarantee of
Creation
Pain can be destructive
It can be productive
It is difficult to predict

Compassion exhales fragrance
And it is unmistakable
Compassion is never barren
It has effects, no aftereffects
It is inbuilt
It is only about affirmations
Compassion is its own creator

Alphabet-formed words
Require boundaries
To be glorified as literature
Or certified as knowledge

What is created out of fervour
Is free, unrestricted
It travels beyond horizons

It is ongoing
All around
And collective in destination

Compassion is inclusive
Of everyone's dreams
In my experience
Compassion is the root of creation

When pain is moderate
Compassion is modest
When pain becomes suffering
Compassion becomes passion
And when its presence, potency, severity
Becomes unbearable
Compassion unwittingly
Transforms into creation

Yes, at times
Anguish is capable of suffocating
Compassion
That's because
Compassion disapproves of struggle

My only plea to you, Mother
Is to bestow me with patience
That someday
The existing darkness dispels
Someday
The ongoing conflict ceases
Someday
Enlightenment will prevail

CONSTANT CONFLICT

1ST JANUARY 1987

All over the universe today
People are celebrating the New Year
Man needs celebrations
To ignite life with energy
The annual celebration is a reflection
Of a restricted thought process
And to every year
Wait anxiously for this day
Is in itself a contradiction

Frankly isn't every New Year
Nature's way of drawing us closer
To our end
Aren't we proceeding, or being compelled
To proceed towards
The ultimate finishing line?

Granted this mystery is only
For those who believe
That death swallows him
Who flees death!

And challenges those
Who defy death!

Yes, some desire death
To dissolve in light
Some submit to it
To attain enlightenment

This awakening in itself
Is a state of mind
That enables one to
Experience what occurs
Also, what does not

Our preoccupation with acquisition
Emerges from the darkness within
That's when we resort to devotion
And pray to the Mother Goddess

I plead that what I endure
Or for whatever reasons I endure

If I am deprived of the shining light
Then what?

Then
My only plea to you, mother
Is to bestow me with patience
That someday
The existing darkness dispels
Someday
The ongoing conflict ceases
Someday
Enlightenment will prevail

We envision
A life of contentment
Not as ambition
But as submission
The joy of restraint
Is a different pinnacle
The joy of sacrifice
The joy of surrender
The joy of endurance

SACRIFICE AND FULFILMENT

We have saturated
All deliberations
On the East vs. the West
Technology has long ago
Demolished emotions
And yet
We are unable
To contain ourselves
Unable to accept
The supremacy of the West
Unable to expand
Our horizons

We live within
Our narrow walls
Unable to obtain
Unable to offer
And what persists
Unable to endure
Unable to absorb
Isn't that irony?

Let's not assume that
Circumstances
Spring out of the blue
Man is self-centred
He looks to convenience self
It is difficult for such people
To empathize with others
And they are therefore
Seldom content

They crave every moment
For more and more
Something new,
Something different
The desire to obtain
Is constant, intense
Perhaps a philosophy
Borrowed from the West

Back home, we envision
A life of contentment

Not as ambition
But as submission
The joy of restraint
Is a different pinnacle
The joy of sacrifice
The joy of surrender
The joy of endurance
Only such joy
Breeds fulfilment
And musters courage
To stand by convictions
In adversities

If not
The energies get scattered
There's no way of preserving them
They are on the road to devastation!
Thought for introspection
But it somehow leaves me untouched

It is acceptable
That you don't have expectations

But unacceptable
That you only think of self

How does one imagine
A life without submission?
There is an old saying:
What is mine is mine
And I hold a share in yours too
What does this reflect?

Wisdom says since expectations
Never extinguish
They can be weighed into words
In a way that adds value to it
That's the beauty of life
And it sets self apart from others

Probably the following lines
Are dedicated to the same thought:

I do my thing and you do your thing,
I am not in this world

To live up to your expectation
And you are not in this world
To live up to mine
You are you and I am I
And if by chance we find each other
It is beautiful

About the Author

Narendra Damodardas Modi was born in Vadnagar, a small town in north Gujarat, on 17 September 1950, the third child in a humble, underprivileged family. His father, Damodardas, ran a tea shop near the Vadnagar station and his mother Heeraben worked as a domestic help in the neighbourhood to earn a living. A mediocre student, Narendra was a voracious reader and from childhood was fascinated by the social cause and Sanyasta. At an early age he went to the Himalayas to search for the meaning of life. Deciding that his inner calling was not to renounce the world but to contribute to the well-being of his fellow humans, he returned home and then joined the Rashtriya Swayamsevak Sangh where he became a Pracharak. He was included in the Gujarat cadre of the Bharatiya Janata Party in 1988; he became the General Secretary of the Gujarat BJP in 1990, and subsequently the All-India General Secretary. On 7 October 2002, he took oath as the chief minister of Gujarat and continued in the post till 2014. He became prime minister of India on 26 May 2014. He was elected to a second term in May 2019 and a third term in June 2024.

ABOUT THE TRANSLATOR

Bhawana Somaaya has been a film critic for almost forty years and has contributed columns to various publications. She has authored several books on cinema. Her books are a point of reference for students studying cinema at Whistling Woods, Manipal University and Jawaharlal Nehru University. She has served on the advisory panel of CBFC India and the governing council of FTII, Pune, is the chairperson of the Tigerland India Film Festival, Madhya Pradesh and on the board of Dhai Akshar, an NGO. She is currently the Entertainment Editor at the 92.7 Big FM radio channel. She was conferred the Padma Shri in 2017.

HarperCollins *Publishers* India

At HarperCollins India, we believe in telling the best stories and finding the widest readership for our books in every format possible. We started publishing in 1992; a great deal has changed since then, but what has remained constant is the passion with which our authors write their books, the love with which readers receive them, and the sheer joy and excitement that we as publishers feel in being a part of the publishing process.

Over the years, we've had the pleasure of publishing some of the finest writing from the subcontinent and around the world, including several award-winning titles and some of the biggest bestsellers in India's publishing history. But nothing has meant more to us than the fact that millions of people have read the books we published, and that somewhere, a book of ours might have made a difference.

As we look to the future, we go back to that one word—a word which has been a driving force for us all these years.

Read.

Harper Collins 4th HARPER FICTION HARPER NON-FICTION HARPER BUSINESS HarperCollins *Children's Books*

HARPER DESIGN Harper Sport HARPER PERENNIAL HARPER VANTAGE हार्पर हिन्दी